The
Dred Scott Decision

by Jason Skog

Content Adviser: Gregg Ivers, Ph.D.,
Department of Government,
American University

Reading Adviser: Katie Van Sluys, Ph.D.,
School of Education
DePaul University

COMPASS POINT BOOKS
MINNEAPOLIS, MINNESOTA

Compass Point Books
3109 West 50th Street, #115
Minneapolis, MN 55410

Visit Compass Point Books on the Internet at *www.compasspointbooks.com*
or e-mail your request to *custserv@compasspointbooks.com*

On the cover: Portrait of Dred Scott over 1875 title page of *The Case of Dred Scott*

Photographs ©: North Wind Picture Archives, cover (bottom left), 5, 6, 11, 41; Courtesy of Georgetown Book Shop, cover background; Prints Old & Rare, back cover (far left); Library of Congress, back cover, 8, 9, 18, 28 (top), 30, 33; Detail of *Dred Scott* by Louis Schultze, Missouri Historical Society Art Collection, photograph by David Schultz/Missouri Historical Society, St. Louis, 12; Smithsonian American Art Museum, Washington, D.C./Art Resource, N.Y., 13; Minnesota Historical Society/artist John Casper Wild, 15; David Muench/Corbis, 16; Al Fenn/Time Life Pictures/Getty Images, 20; St. Louis Circuit Court Historical Records Projects/Washington University in St. Louis, 21, 22; Photographs and Prints Collection/ Missouri Historical Society, St. Louis, 23, 27; Photographs and Prints Collection, daguerreotype by Thomas M. Easterly, photograph by Dennis Waters/Missouri Historical Society, St. Louis, 25; The Granger Collection, New York, 28 (bottom), 31; Our Documents/National Archives and Records Administration, 29, 38; Bettmann/Corbis, 37.

Managing Editor: Catherine Neitge
Page Production: Noumenon Creative
Photo Researcher: Svetlana Zhurkin
Cartographer: XNR Productions, Inc.
Library Consultant: Kathleen Baxter

Creative Director: Keith Griffin
Editorial Director: Carol Jones

Library of Congress Cataloging-in-Publication Data
Skog, Jason.
  The Dred Scott Decision/ by Jason Skog.
    p. cm.—(We the people)
  Includes bibliographical references and index.
  ISBN-13: 978-0-7565-2026-7 (hardcover)
  ISBN-10: 0-7565-2026-6 (hardcover)
  ISBN-13: 978-0-7565-2038-0 (paperback)
  ISBN-10: 0-7565-2038-X (paperback)
  1. Scott, Dred, 1809–1858—Trials, litigation, etc. 2. Sanford, John F.A., 1806-or 7–1857—Trials, litigation, etc. 3. Slavery—United States—Legal status of slaves in free states. 4. Slavery—Law and legislation—United States—History. 5. Scott, Dred, 1809–1858. 6. Slavery—Law and legislation.
  I. Title. II. Series: We the people (Series) (Compass Point Books)
    KF228.S27S556 2004
    342.7308'7—dc22   2006006765

TABLE OF CONTENTS

THE RULING

It was a cool, sunny morning in Washington, D.C., on March 6, 1857. The courtroom deep within the nation's Capitol was crammed with curious spectators and members of the press. Whispers went through the crowd as the nine justices in black robes entered the room at 11 A.M. The audience and the nation were eager to hear the Supreme Court's ruling on whether a slave named Dred Scott was a free man.

Slavery had been a common practice in the United States since its earliest days. Most slaves had originally been brought to the United States from Africa against their will. Men, women, and children—some of whom were separated from their parents—were rounded up, chained, and stacked like lumber on ships for their voyage to America. Many slaves died of disease during their journey, and their bodies were thrown overboard. When the ships ran low on food, many of the living were thrown overboard as well.

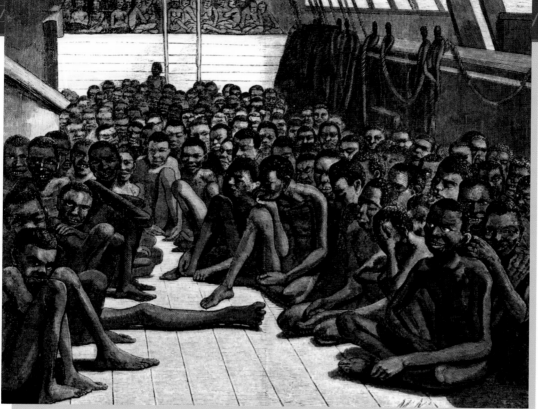

Kidnapped Africans were packed into slave ships and taken to America.

Those who survived the voyage were sold once they were in the United States, and their descendants were born into slavery and remained slaves. They were forced to work long hours for no pay. Enslaved people often lived in terrible conditions from which they could not escape, and many were abused by their masters.

By the early 1800s, states in the North had banned slavery through their state constitutions. States in the South

5

Slaves were forced to work long hours on cotton plantations in the South.

still allowed it. The issue was threatening to divide the country. While Congress had been debating slavery for years, it hadn't settled the question of slavery in the federal territories. These territories were lands owned by the government that were not yet states.

Through various laws and compromises during the first half of the 19th century, Congress had taken different actions regarding slavery. It sometimes banned slavery in federal territories; it sometimes allowed slavery in federal

territories; and it sometimes left it up to the citizens of a territory to decide.

For example, the Missouri Compromise of 1820 allowed Missouri to enter the Union as a slave state. But it banned slavery in certain federal territory north of Missouri's border. In 1854, Congress reversed that decision and allowed slavery in territory where it had been banned by the Missouri Compromise. And now, in 1857, the Supreme Court was about to decide Dred Scott's fate, along with the fate of slaves throughout the country.

Neither Scott nor John F.A. Sanford—the man Scott was fighting for his freedom—was in the courtroom for the announcement that morning. Scott was still a slave working in St. Louis, Missouri, 11 years after he first filed suit claiming he was a free man. Sanford was in a hospital for the mentally ill and would die just two months later. But both men were much smaller than the issue at stake and were now just bit players in a much bigger battle.

Chief Justice Roger B. Taney, who was nearly 80

Roger B. Taney (1777–1864)

years old, held the court's decision in his trembling hands and began to read. His reading of the decision lasted two hours. Then other judges on the court read their opinions of the decision, some agreeing and some disagreeing with the majority. When it was all over the next day, their ruling was final. By a vote of 7 to 2, the Supreme Court decided that Scott and his family were still slaves.

But the court's decision had a much wider effect than just on Dred Scott. The court's interpretation of the laws resulted in two major findings: First, that no person of African ancestry, whether free in the North or enslaved in the South, could be a U.S. citizen; and second, that Congress could not ban slavery in the federal territories, and any attempt to do so would be unconstitutional.

The men who drafted the Constitution, wrote Justice Taney, believed that blacks "had no rights which the white man was bound to respect; and that the negro might justly and lawfully be reduced to slavery for his benefit. He was bought and sold and treated as an ordinary article of merchandise and traffic, whenever profit could be made by it."

Many people believe that the decision was the low point of the Supreme Court's long history. It put the entire future of black Americans in doubt and pushed the country toward the Civil War, a bloody four-year conflict that nearly tore the nation in two.

NOW READY:
THE
Dred Scott Decision.

OPINION OF CHIEF-JUSTICE ROGER B. TANEY,
WITH AN INTRODUCTION,
BY DR. J. H. VAN EVRIE.

ALSO,
AN APPENDIX,
By SAM. A. CARTWRIGHT, M.D., of New Orleans,
ENTITLED,

"Natural History of the Prognathous Race of Mankind."
ORIGINALLY WRITTEN FOR THE NEW YORK DAY-BOOK.

THE GREAT WANT OF A BRIEF PAMPHLET, containing the famous decision of Chief-Justice Taney, in the celebrated Dred Scott Case, has induced the Publishers of the DAY-BOOK to present this edition to the public. It contains a Historical Introduction by Dr. Van Evrie, author of "Negroes and Negro Slavery," and an Appendix by Dr. Cartwright, of New Orleans, in which the physical differences between the negro and the white races are forcibly presented. As a whole, this pamphlet gives the *historical*, *legal*, and *physical* aspects of the "Slavery" Question in a concise compass, and should be circulated by thousands before the next presidential election. All who desire to answer the arguments of the abolitionists should read it. In order to place it before the masses, and induce Democratic Clubs, Democratic Town Committees, and all interested in the cause, to order it for distribution, it has been put down at the following low rates, for which it will be sent, free of postage, to any part of the United States. Dealers supplied at the same rate.

Single Copies $0 25
Five Copies 1 00
Twelve Copies 2 00
Fifty Copies 7 00
One Hundred Copies 12 00
Every additional Hundred.......... 10 00

Address
VAN EVRIE, HORTON, & CO.,
Publishers of DAY-BOOK,
No. 40 Ann Street, New York.

An 1859 pamphlet used Justice Taney's arguments to support slavery.

EARLY YEARS

While the case made Dred Scott one of the nation's most famous slaves, little is known about his personal life, especially his younger years.

The story of his long struggle toward freedom began in 1830, with the arrival of Peter Blow and his wife, Elizabeth, in the busy river port of St. Louis, Missouri. The white couple had three daughters, four sons, and six slaves. Blow once owned plantations in Virginia and Alabama, but he wanted to do something other than farming. He started a hotel in St. Louis, but it wasn't very successful. His wife died just a year after they arrived, and by 1832, his own health began to fail and he soon died. Of Blow's six slaves, one was sold while Blow was still alive and another was sold after his death to settle a debt.

Around that time, a U.S. Army surgeon named John Emerson of St. Louis arrived at Fort Armstrong in Illinois, a state that banned slavery. With him was his slave

Fort Armstrong stood on Rock Island where the Rock and Mississippi rivers meet.

named Dred Scott, who was once owned by Peter Blow. It's unclear whether Scott was the slave Blow sold before or after his death.

It is also unknown if Dred Scott was born with that name or if he was given it later in life. He had been with the Blow family since he was a boy and would stay in touch

11

with the Blows until his death. Scott, born in Virginia in 1799, had dark skin and stood less than 5 feet (150 centimeters) tall. Newspapers described him as "illiterate but not ignorant," meaning he couldn't read but he wasn't stupid. They also described him as having "strong common sense" and being well-traveled.

There are few other details about his personality, his abilities, or his relationships. But the slave Dr. Emerson owned was the same man who went on to file the suit that became the famous Supreme Court case of *Dred Scott v. Sandford*. It is also unclear how much of the 11-year lawsuit was Scott's idea. Though many have said he played only a small role, it's clear he very much wanted to be free.

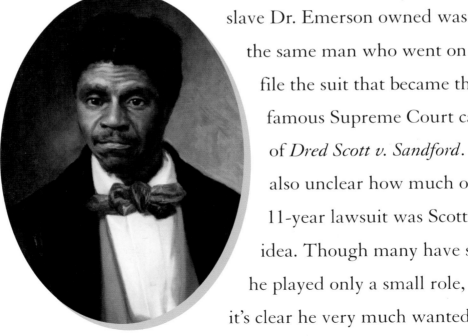

Dred Scott (1799–1858)

12

FROM TOWN TO TOWN

Dr. Emerson often complained about his own working
conditions and regularly asked to work somewhere else. In
1836, he was sent to Fort Snelling in St. Paul, Minnesota,
and he took Scott with him. At the time, St. Paul was part
of the Wisconsin Territory, an area that banned slavery.
By now, Scott had been held as a slave in the free state

The Dakota camped near Fort Snelling in the early days of the fort.

13

of Illinois for two years and was now living in a federal territory that also did not allow slavery.

During his time at Fort Snelling, Scott met his future wife, Harriet Robinson. She was about half his age and also a slave. The two were married in a civil ceremony by Major Lawrence Taliaferro, an Indian agent and justice of the peace. Taliaferro was also Harriet's owner. Her ownership was then transferred to Emerson. The Scotts' marriage lasted for more than 20 years, until Dred Scott died. Of their four children, two sons died when they were infants. But their two daughters, Eliza and Lizzie, survived and became part of the famous lawsuit.

By the spring of 1837, Emerson decided winters at Fort Snelling were too cold. He again asked for a new post, and Army officials in Washington agreed to send him back to Jefferson Barracks in St. Louis. Emerson left the Scotts at Fort Snelling, planning to send for them later. But when Emerson got to St. Louis, his orders were changed, and he was sent instead to Fort Jesup in western

Fort Snelling overlooks the junction of the Minnesota and Mississippi rivers.

Louisiana. Two days after his arrival there, he was already complaining and asked to go back to Fort Snelling.

He didn't get to leave for more than a year. During his stay at Fort Jesup, Emerson met a woman named Eliza Irene Sanford, who was known as Irene. She was visiting

Fort Jesup with her sister, whose husband was an Army captain there. On February 6, 1838, John Emerson and Irene Sanford married. When spring came, Emerson sent

The Mississippi River flowed through slave territory and free territory.

for Dred and Harriet Scott. The Scotts were still at Fort Snelling, working for other Army officers. They traveled by steamboat to Fort Jesup but didn't stay long. By September, Emerson got another transfer and took his wife and the Scotts back to Fort Snelling. They all took a boat from Fort Jesup to St. Louis, where they boarded the steamboat *Gypsy* and headed north on the Mississippi River toward Fort Snelling.

The Scotts' journey was significant for two reasons. First, they were again going to live in territory that banned slavery. Second, Harriet Scott gave birth to a child onboard the boat in an area that banned slavery. As the *Gypsy* paddled up the Mississippi River toward St. Paul, a baby girl—named Eliza, after Emerson's wife—was born.

Things did not go smoothly for Emerson at Fort Snelling. He got into several fights and arguments with other officers. By the spring of 1840, Emerson was sent to work in Florida, where the Seminole War was taking place. When he left Fort Snelling, Emerson stopped in

17

St. Louis to drop off his wife and the Scott family.

Florida didn't suit Emerson either. In August 1842, he started complaining again to his bosses at the surgeon general's office. This time, it seemed they had had enough of his whining. Army orders to cut back on the medical staff gave Emerson's bosses a chance to get rid of him. Emerson got an honorable dismissal from the service.

Upon leaving the Army, Emerson moved his still growing family to Davenport, near land he owned in the

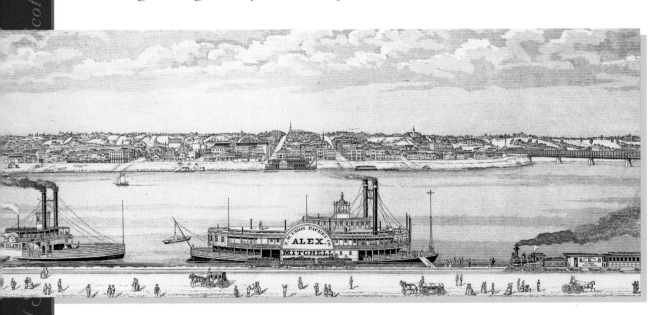

Davenport, Iowa, was settled along the Mississippi River.

Iowa Territory. Soon after arriving there, Irene Emerson gave birth to a baby girl named Henrietta. It is not known whether the Scotts came along, but it is considered unlikely since slavery was strictly banned in the Iowa Territory. It is also thought that the Emersons would not have needed slaves since they were living in a hotel while their new home was being built. Shortly after their move and the birth of his daughter, Dr. Emerson prepared a will—a legal document showing who would receive his property and money when he died. He signed the will on December 29, 1843, and unexpectedly died later that night. He was about 40 years old.

The will and the time Dred Scott spent with the Emersons became significant factors in the legal battles to come. Almost all of Emerson's property was given to his wife, Irene. Upon her death, it was to be transferred to their daughter. Irene's brother, John F.A. Sanford of St. Louis, was one of the executors of Emerson's will, meaning he was in charge of the estate and of selling

Harriet and Dred Scott fought a long battle for their freedom.

any of Emerson's property that was necessary, including his slaves. That duty would later connect him to Dred Scott's Supreme Court case.

After Emerson's death, Dred and Harriet Scott were loaned to a family in Texas before returning to St. Louis in 1846 to work for another family. Soon after, the Scotts began their efforts to become free citizens.

FIGHT FOR FREEDOM

On April 6, 1846, Dred and Harriet Scott filed papers in a Missouri circuit court explaining that they had previously lived on free land. As residents of Missouri, a slave state, they needed permission to sue Irene Emerson to establish their freedom. The judge granted their request. In his papers, Scott stated that Mrs. Emerson had "beat, bruised and ill-treated him" before holding him like a prisoner for 12 hours. He also claimed to be a "free person" held as a slave and requested payment of $10. Harriet Scott filed similar papers. Since they couldn't write, Dred and Harriet Scott each signed their paper with

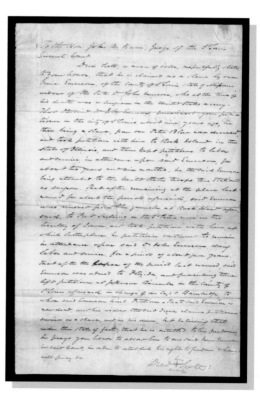

The Scotts' petition to sue for freedom was filed on April 6, 1846.

Dred Scott's mark is among the court papers preserved by the state of Missouri.

their mark, an X, and the two lawsuits were considered together through the Missouri courts.

How the Scotts came to decide to use the legal system to fight for freedom remains a mystery. It is unclear who helped them get started. It's possible Dred Scott thought of it himself. He was well-traveled, and such suits were often discussed among slaves in St. Louis. Most likely, his decision came out of talks he had with members of the Blow family, whom he had known since he was a boy.

Many lawyers helped the Scotts with their case, most of them working for free or for very little money. Those lawyers and others who knew about Missouri law felt the Scotts had a strong case.

Charles Drake, a relative of the Blow family, helped with the case.

Missouri's highest court, the state supreme court, had been favoring slaves whose masters had taken them to free states. But the Scott case took a long time to move through the courts because of strong opposition by Irene Emerson, her lawyers, and other people supporting her.

Public opinion on slavery in Missouri was changing, along with how judges were looking at such cases. The Scotts would soon find themselves caught up in tensions between the Northern and Southern states over slavery.

In their first trial, the Scotts lost on a technicality. Their lawyers appealed and were granted a new trial. But Emerson's attorneys objected to this ruling, and the case was sent to the Missouri Supreme Court. The state's highest court ruled that the Scotts deserved to be heard again, and they were granted a fresh start. But the couple's desire to be free was matched by Emerson's wish to keep them as slaves. Her defense team's actions showed she wanted to win however she could.

In 1848, Emerson's brother, John Sanford, took over the supervision of his sister's estate. He also hired a new lawyer to handle her defense of the case, which went to trial again in 1850. This time, testimony from a key witness made it clear Emerson was the Scotts' owner. Still, a judge ruled that the Scotts were free.

But the battle wasn't over. Emerson's lawyers took the case back to the Missouri Supreme Court, but the court put off hearing it. A decision wasn't made until March 1852, and by then the country was in a bitter struggle over

The Missouri Supreme Court met in the St. Louis Courthouse.

slavery. Southerners felt their way of life was under attack. Northerners were speaking louder than ever about their opposition to slavery. As a slave state bordered by the free states of Iowa and Illinois, Missouri was stuck in the middle of it all.

25

In a 2-1 vote, the Missouri Supreme Court over-turned the lower court's decision, ruling that Scott was still a slave and so was his wife, Harriet. The court said that every state had a right to enforce its own laws and ignore the laws from other states if they disagreed. In other words, Missouri residents could do what they wanted with their slaves, even if that meant taking them to free states.

At the end of 1853, Scott had new lawyers and appeared to be the property of a new owner. By then, he had been sold to John Sanford, Emerson's brother. It could have been that Sanford was simply trying to protect his sister from the ongoing legal dispute. Whatever the reason for his new ownership of the Scotts, Sanford was the person who later became the defendant in the famous U.S. Supreme Court case.

Meanwhile, Scott took a different route in his fight for freedom, this time suing Sanford in federal court, rather than state court. That case went to trial on May 15, 1854. Again, things did not go well for Scott.

26

The judge told the jury that the law was on Sanford's side and said Missouri could make its own laws regarding slavery, just as the Missouri Supreme Court had found. The jury agreed and ruled in favor of John Sanford.

Roswell Field worked on the Scotts' case for free.

After Scott's lawyer failed to get a new trial, he filed papers that were the first step toward taking the case to the U.S. Supreme Court. But before the Scotts could take their case to the highest court in the land, they would need a new lawyer. They needed one who was comfortable arguing the case in such a charged atmosphere. And they would need him to work for free or for very little money.

On Christmas Eve 1854, a lawyer who had been handling the Scotts' case wrote a letter to Montgomery Blair,

27

Montgomery Blair

Reverdy Johnson

asking for help. Blair was a successful Washington lawyer who had appeared before the Supreme Court and had once practiced law in St. Louis. After talking with his family, Blair agreed to take on the Scott case without pay. George T. Curtis, a noted lawyer from Massachusetts and the brother of Supreme Court Justice Benjamin R. Curtis, also joined the defense team.

Handling Sanford's defense were two prominent lawyers, both with pro-slavery connections. Henry S. Geyer was a U.S. senator and respected Missouri lawyer, and Reverdy Johnson was a former senator and one of the most respected constitutional lawyers in the country.

The Scott case was formally filed in the U.S. Supreme Court on December 30, 1854, but there were many cases in line ahead of it. It would be more than a year before the court paid any attention to the Scotts' case. The public also was unaware of the case and its potential effect on the nation. Very little had been written in the newspapers before the case reached the U.S. Supreme Court, and nothing was reported even when it was filed. In addition, antislavery activists had failed to take up Dred Scott's cause, something that still puzzles historians.

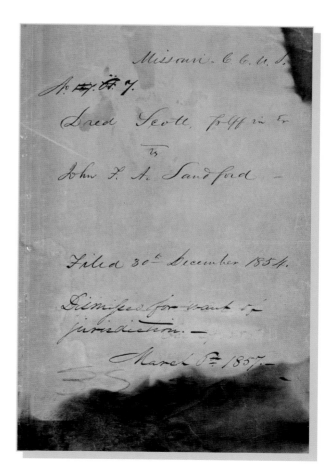

The Dred Scott case was filed in 1854.

ARGUMENTS BEGIN

Arguments before the court began on February 11, 1856. There were technical parts of the case that caused not only uncertainties but another delay. The case was held over for another round of arguments the following December. Some worried the delays were the result of political motives. One of the justices was accused of trying to use the case to get a presidential nomination. Even Abraham

Lincoln, who would run for president four years later, said the court was delaying because some politicians were trying to hide their pro-slavery positions. Most likely, however, the justices didn't want to make such a controversial decision during an election year. The recently formed

Abraham Lincoln

Republican Party opposed the spread of slavery to the territories. The Democrats preferred to leave slavery decisions to the states and territories themselves.

By the time the second round of Supreme Court arguments got under way, many more people were aware of what was at stake in one slave's pursuit of freedom. The arguments were attended by prominent judges, members of Congress, and the press. Twelve hours of arguments went on over four days.

SUPREME COURT OF THE UNITED STATES.

No. 7.—DECEMBER TERM, 1856.

DRED SCOTT, (A COLORED MAN,)

vs.

JOHN F. A. SANDFORD.

Argument of Montgomery Blair, of Counsel for the Plaintiff in Error.

STATEMENT OF THE CASE.

This is a suit brought to try the right to freedom of the plaintiff and his wife Harriet, and his children Eliza and Lizzie. It was originally brought against the administratrix of Dr. Emerson, in the circuit court of St. Louis county, Missouri, where the plaintiff recovered judgment; but on appeal to the supreme court of the State, a majority of that court, at the March term of 1852, reversed the judgment; when the cause was remanded it was dismissed, and this suit, which is an action of trespass for false imprisonment, was brought in the circuit court of the United States for the district of Missouri, by the plaintiff, as a "citizen" of that State, against the defendant, a "citizen" of the State of New York, who had purchased him and his family since the commencement of the suit in the State court.

The defendant denied, by plea in abatement, the jurisdiction of the circuit court of the United States, on the ground that the plaintiff "is a negro of African descent, his ancestors were of pure African blood, and were brought into this country and sold as slaves," and therefore the plaintiff "is not a citizen of the State of Missouri." To this plea the plaintiff demurred, and the court sustained the demurrer.

Thereupon the defendant pleaded over, and justified the trespass on the ground that the plaintiff and his family were his negro slaves; and a statement of facts, agreed to by both parties, was read in evidence, as follows: "In the year 1834, the plaintiff was a negro slave belonging

First page of the printed argument put before the Supreme Court by Montgomery Blair

On the question of whether Scott was a citizen, Blair, his lawyer, cited state and federal laws where *citizen* meant "free inhabitant." He argued that blacks of African descent should be considered citizens under the Constitution. And though they didn't yet have the right to vote or serve on juries, Blair argued that they at least qualified as "quasi-citizens," meaning they could own property, conduct business, and sue in the court system.

Speaking for Sanford, Geyer suggested that Scott should not have been allowed to take his case to the federal courts because he needed to be a citizen of the United States in order to do so. He went on to say that citizens become so either by birth or by naturalization. And since Scott had been born a slave, he could not be considered a citizen or even a quasi-citizen. Geyer also said that even if Scott's trips with Dr. Emerson into free territory made him a free man, they didn't also make him a U.S. citizen. It became a line of logic that Chief Justice Taney would eventually follow.

Arguments then moved on to Scott's time in Illinois. Sanford's lawyers argued that Emerson, as a member of the Army, was merely a visitor there rather than a resident of the state. But Scott's lawyers countered by saying that at no time during his travels did Emerson claim to be a resident anywhere

FRANK LESLIE'S ILLUSTRATED NEWSPAPER

Entered according to Act of Congress, in the year 1857, by FRANK LESLIE, in the Clerk's Office of the District Court for the Southern District of New York. (Copyrighted June 22, 1857.)

No. 82.—VOL. IV.]   NEW YORK, SATURDAY, JUNE 27, 1857.   [PRICE 6 CENTS.

TO TOURISTS AND TRAVELLERS.

We shall be happy to receive personal narratives, of land or sea, including adventures and incidents, from every person who pleases to correspond with our paper.

We take this opportunity of returning our thanks to our numerous artistic correspondents throughout the country, for the many sketches we are constantly receiving from them of the news of the day. We trust they will spare no pains to furnish us with drawings of events as they occur. We would also remind them that it is necessary to send all sketches, if possible, by the earliest conveyance.

VISIT TO DRED SCOTT—HIS FAMILY—INCIDENTS OF HIS LIFE—DECISION OF THE SUPREME COURT.

While standing in the Fair grounds at St. Louis, and engaged in conversation with a prominent citizen of that enterprising city, he suddenly asked us if we would not like to be introduced to Dred Scott. Upon expressing a desire to be thus honored, the gentleman called to an old negro who was standing near by, and our wish was gratified. Dred made a rude obeisance to our recognition, and seemed to enjoy the notice we expended upon him. We found him on examination to be a pure-blooded African, perhaps fifty years of age, with a shrewd, intelligent, good-natured face, of rather light frame, being not more than five feet six inches high. After some general remarks we expressed a wish to get his portrait (we had made

ELIZA AND LIZZIE, CHILDREN OF DRED SCOTT.

efforts before, through correspondents, and failed), and asked him if he would not go to Fitzgibbon's gallery and

have it taken. The gentleman present explained to Dred that it was proper he should have his likeness in the "great illustrated paper of the country," over-ruled his many objections, which seemed to grow out of a superstitious feeling, and he promised to be at the gallery the next day. This appointment Dred did not keep. Determined not to be foiled, we sought an interview with Mr. Crane, Dred's lawyer, who promptly gave us a letter of introduction, explaining to Dred that it was to his advantage to have his picture taken and to be engraved for our paper, and also directions where we could find his domicile. We found the place with difficulty, the streets in Dred's neighborhood being more closely defined in the plan of the city than on the mother earth; we finally reached a wooden house, however, protected by a balcony that answered the description. Approaching the door, we saw a smart, tidy-looking negress, perhaps thirty years of age, who, with two female assistants, was busy ironing. To our question, "Is this where Dred Scott lives?" we received, rather hesitatingly, the answer, "Yes." Upon our asking if he was home, she said,

The Dred Scott *case was covered by* Frank Leslie's Illustrated Newspaper *in 1857.*

other than where he was living at the time.

They went on to argue that the Missouri court ignored its own precedent by ruling against Scott and made a decision purely for political reasons. In the past, Missouri courts had regularly ruled in favor of slaves who sued for their freedom after being taken to free states. For the Missouri Supreme Court to suddenly change its mind

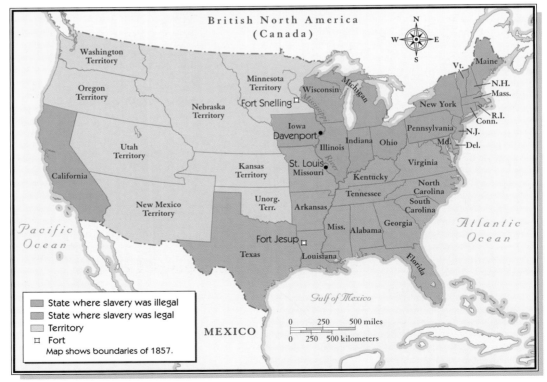

Dred Scott had lived in both free and slave states.

and ignore Illinois' antislavery laws was improper, Scott's lawyers argued. But Chief Justice Taney had ruled in an earlier case that state judges could find another state's laws "repugnant" and choose not to follow them. That thinking also seemed to support Sanford's defense.

There was little discussion about the time Scott had lived at Fort Snelling. As part of a federal territory, slavery was not allowed at Fort Snelling. But Sanford's legal team took a different approach about this. They suggested the Missouri Compromise—the law banning slavery in northern federal territories—was unconstitutional. The abrupt turn in arguments suddenly made the Missouri Compromise of 1820 a central focus of the *Scott* case.

While the legal arguments were sometimes complicated and perhaps boring, interest in the case and the debate around it reached a peak. Members of Congress were angrily debating the same subject in the same building, and the American public was eager for the outcome.

FINAL DECISION

Despite hopes for a quick decision, another series of delays followed. Finally, two months later, on February 14, 1857, the Supreme Court justices gathered to discuss the arguments they had heard. Seven of the nine justices had been appointed to the court by pro-slavery presidents. Five of the justices were from the South, and there was a lot of pressure from people in their home states to keep slavery alive. A decision for slavery, they thought, would help quiet the criticism and discrimination many slave owners were getting from the North. There also was pressure from President-elect James Buchanan, a Democrat who was hoping for an answer before he delivered his inaugural address to an anxious nation. The answer came two days after Buchanan was sworn in as president.

Chief Justice Taney, who was a strong supporter of slavery, was chosen to write the opinion for the majority. Taney had grown up in a wealthy Maryland family that

James Buchanan was inaugurated shortly before a court decision was reached.

owned slaves who worked on the family's tobacco plantation. In addition, Taney had decided against enslaved people in the past. In an earlier Supreme Court case, he had ruled in favor of fugitive slave laws, which said

37

escaped slaves must be returned to their owners, even if they were found in free states in the North.

After Justice Taney read the majority opinion on March 6 to a packed courtroom over the course of several hours, one thing was perfectly clear: Dred Scott was still a slave. Taney wrote that African-Americans were "beings of an inferior order ... so far inferior, that they had no rights which the white man was bound to respect."

The Supreme Court ruling meant blacks were not citizens and, therefore, could not bring suit in a federal court. It also denied Congress the power to prohibit slavery in the federal territories.

Justice Taney's judgment in the Dred Scott case.

38

PUBLIC REACTION

The *Dred Scott* decision drew fast and harsh reaction from the North, where antislavery activists spoke the loudest. Some newspaper editorials said the Supreme Court justices used the same kind of wisdom and logic that was found in "any Washington barroom." The *New York Tribune* called the decision "atrocious," "wicked," and "abominable."

Among Southerners, the court's ruling gave them the satisfaction that their ways were upheld by the Constitution. Others seemed relieved that the court had finally settled an explosive issue and urged people to accept the decision. While it may have been the last word from the court at the time, the ruling didn't stop the bitter conflict between North and South on the subject of slavery.

And, as it turned out, the public's reaction was much louder and stronger than the actual legal impact. While the new law seemed to support and encourage slavery, the use of slaves never really expanded. But the infamous decision

39

nudged an already divided nation closer and closer to the bloody Civil War.

Shortly after the Supreme Court decision, Irene Emerson transferred Dred Scott and his family back to the Blow family. Emerson's new husband, Calvin C. Chaffee, was a Northern congressman who opposed slavery. The Blows set the Scotts free in May 1857, and their days of slavery were over. But 16 months later, Dred Scott was dead. He died of tuberculosis on September 17, 1858.

Four years later, in the midst of the Civil War, President Abraham Lincoln issued the Emancipation Proclamation. It said that enslaved people in the rebellious South were free. But its full effects weren't felt until the end of the war in 1865. That same year, Congress passed the 13th Amendment to the Constitution, banning slavery. The next year, Congress passed the Civil Rights Act of 1866, which gave former slaves the right to own property and to bring suit in federal court.

The 13th Amendment had the direct effect of over-

African-Americans celebrated the passage of the Civil Rights Act of 1866.

ruling the *Dred Scott* decision. The 1866 law carried those new rights into effect.

More than 4 million people were no longer enslaved. They were free.

GLOSSARY

abominable—causing disgust or hatred

estate—a deceased person's property or money

executors—people in charge of overseeing a will, which is a legal document showing how a person's estate should be divided up after his or her death

Missouri Compromise—an 1820 agreement between pro-slavery and antislavery states concerning the extension of slavery into U.S. territories; it admitted Missouri as a slave state but banned slavery in lands acquired in the Louisiana Purchase north of the 36 degrees 30 minutes line of latitude, which is Missouri's southern border

naturalization—process for a person to become a citizen of a country other than the one in which he or she was born

precedent—an earlier decision by a court that's used to help guide future rulings

unconstitutional—a law that goes against something set forth in the Constitution, the document that set up the government of the United States

DID YOU KNOW?

- It was illegal to campaign against slavery in slave-holding states. It was also against the law to have antislavery literature there.

- Some antislavery preachers read the U.S. Supreme Court's *Dred Scott* decision in church and openly criticized it in front of their congregations.

- Dred Scott was buried in St. Louis Wesleyan Cemetery, which later was overtaken by the city's expansion. His body was moved to Calvary Cemetery in 1867. Then, 90 years later in observance of the Supreme Court decision, the grave was marked by a headstone donated by Peter Blow's great-granddaughter. There is a headstone there for Harriet Robinson Scott, too, but she is not buried there. Her grave, once thought to be lost forever, was recently discovered. She died in 1876 and was buried in Greenwood Cemetery in north St. Louis County, Missouri.

- Later rulings by the U.S. Supreme Court and new laws passed by Congress eventually made Chief Justice Roger Taney's Supreme Court decision the most frequently overturned decision in history.

IMPORTANT DATES

Timeline

1846	Dred and Harriet Scott file suit against Eliza Irene Emerson, seeking their freedom.
1847	The court rules in favor of Emerson.
1850	A judge in a second trial rules Scotts are free.
1852	Emerson appeals the decision to the Missouri Supreme Court, which overrules the lower court; Scotts are still slaves.
1853	Scott files suit in federal court, which rules against him in 1854.
1854	Scott appeals to the U.S. Supreme Court.
1857	U.S. Supreme Court rules that the Scotts are still slaves; they are set free by Taylor Blow.
1858	Dred Scott dies.
1863	President Abraham Lincoln issues the Emancipation Proclamation.
1865	U.S. Congress passes the 13th Amendment, banning slavery.
1866	Congress passes the Civil Rights Act of 1866.
1876	Harriet Scott dies.

IMPORTANT PEOPLE

MONTGOMERY BLAIR (1813–1883)

Served as Dred Scott's lawyer before the U.S. Supreme Court; also served as mayor of St. Louis and U.S. postmaster general

BENJAMIN CURTIS (1809–1874)

One of two Supreme Court justices who disagreed in the Dred Scott *case; the other was John McLean of Ohio; after the decision, Curtis resigned from the court in disgust; he later defended President Andrew Johnson in his impeachment trial in 1868*

JOHN F.A. SANFORD (1806–1857)

Dred Scott's owner when the famous Supreme Court case was filed; a clerk misspelled his last name in court papers so the case was permanently listed as Dred Scott v. Sandford; *he suffered a mental breakdown and died in a New York asylum just months after the decision*

ROGER B. TANEY (1777–1864)

Chief justice of the U.S. Supreme Court from 1836 to 1864 who was responsible for writing the explosive decision in the Dred Scott *case; before he came to the Supreme Court, he was a state legislator, Maryland attorney general, U.S. attorney general, and the secretary of the treasury*

45

WANT TO KNOW MORE?

At the Library

January, Brendan. *The Dred Scott Decision*. New York: Children's
Press, 1998.

Katz, William Loren. *Black Pioneers: An Untold Story*. New York:
Atheneum Books for Young Readers, 1999.

Naden, Corinne J., and Rose Blue. *Dred Scott: Person or Property?*
Tarrytown, N.Y.: Benchmark Books, 2005.

Rappaport, Doreen. *No More! Stories and Songs of Slave Resistance*.
Cambridge, Mass.: Candlewick, 2002.

Rossi, Ann. *Freedom Struggle: The Anti-Slavery Movement 1830–1865*.
Washington, D.C.: National Geographic Children's Books, 2005.

On the Web

For more information on the *Dred Scott Decision*, use FactHound
to track down Web sites related to this book.

1. Go to *www.facthound.com*

2. Type in this book ID: 0756520266

3. Click on the *Fetch It* button.

Your trusty FactHound will fetch the best Web sites for you!

On the Road

United States Supreme Court
1 First St. N.E.
Washington, DC 20543
202/479-3211
Exhibits, lectures, and court sessions
of the highest court in the nation

Missouri History Museum
Lindell and DeBaliviere
in Forest Park
St. Louis, MO 63112
314/746-4599
Information on early Missouri
history and the lives of Missourians

Look for more We the People books about this era:

The Assassination of Abraham Lincoln
ISBN 0-7565-0678-6

Battle of the Ironclads
ISBN 0-7565-1628-5

The Carpetbaggers
ISBN 0-7565-0834-7

The Confederate Soldier
ISBN 0-7565-2025-8

The Emancipation Proclamation
ISBN 0-7565-0209-8

Fort Sumter
ISBN 0-7565-1629-3

The Gettysburg Address
ISBN 0-7565-1271-9

Great Women of the Civil War
ISBN 0-7565-0839-8

The Lincoln-Douglas Debates
ISBN 0-7565-1632-3

The Missouri Compromise
ISBN 0-7565-1634-X

The Reconstruction Amendments
ISBN 0-7565-1636-6

Surrender at Appomattox
ISBN 0-7565-1626-9

The Underground Railroad
ISBN 0-7565-0102-4

The Union Soldier
ISBN 0-7565-2030-4

Women of the Confederacy
ISBN 0-7565-2033-9

Women of the Union
ISBN 0-7565-2035-5

A complete list of We the People titles is available on our Web site:
www.compasspointbooks.com

INDEX

About the Author

Jason Skog is a freelance writer in Brooklyn, New York. He has been a newspaper reporter and magazine writer for 12 years, covering criminal and civil courts, government, education, technology, and features. In 2005, he won a Virginia Press Association award for general news writing. This is his first book.